Free Verse Editions
Edited by Jon Thompson

The Miraculous Courageous

Josh Booton

Winner of the New Measure Poetry Prize

Parlor Press
Anderson, South Carolina
www.parlorpress.com

Parlor Press LLC, Anderson, South Carolina, 29621

© 2018 by Parlor Press
All rights reserved.
Printed in the United States of America
S A N: 2 5 4 - 8 8 7 9

Library of Congress Cataloging-in-Publication Data on File

978-1-60235-447-0 (paperback)
978-1-60235-448-7 (PDF)
978-1-60235-466-1 (ePub)

1 2 3 4 5

Cover design by David Blakesley.
Cover image: Coral Garden. © 2017 by DKart at istockphoto.
    com. Used by permission.
Printed on acid-free paper.

Parlor Press, LLC is an independent publisher of scholarly and
trade titles in print and multimedia formats. This book is available
in paperback and ebook formats from Parlor Press on the World
Wide Web at http://www.parlorpress.com or through online and
brick-and-mortar bookstores. For submission information or to
find out about Parlor Press publications, write to Parlor Press,
3015 Brackenberry Drive, Anderson, South Carolina, 29621, or
email editor@parlorpress.com.

*For all the deep sea divers
who've taught me how to chart the sea.*

Contents

Contents

The Miraculous Courageous

The best way to observe a fish is to become a fish.

—Jacques Cousteau

the books all quote my brain is wrong
say a disorder of neural development
say they don't know exactly why
I'm not exactly right they're wrong though
to say disordered when I'm more
ordered than anyone I know I know
sometimes the world is a **trickysituation**
to get just but maybe the world is
wrong sometimes the world that wants
to look me in the eye when I want to
look away when I want to say I know
my life more than you or nothing at all

in my first memory mom is crying
shaking me I don't know why she was
crying but the tears feel **almostnice**
on my cheeks warm and soft and even
the shaking feels nice she is saying
something in my ear but it's too close
to hear only never and love her hair
smells clean covering my face as she
lifts me up carried me into the car
the seatbelt rough against my neck
the stop lights going green yellow red

anthony says seahorses are gay but
really the males just carry the eggs
instead of females anthony doesn't
know much about marine biology
but he'll beat the shit he said out
of anyone who bothers me anthony
likes sharks any of numerous mostly
marine cartilaginous fishes because
they're ridiculously badass with rows
and rows of **razorteeth** and aren't
ever afraid anthony says seahorses
ain't shit and for once he's true

this is where we **shakehands** stare
each other in the eyes three firm shakes
and let go though I don't know why
we don't just figure each other out
from a distance sniff the air for signs
of friendliness the odor of anger which
would be perfect a spray to spray
to keep others away without having to
yell *in the town where I was born lived a man*
who and then the wind after then
carries the scent off and you can choose
another like boredom or happiness
which smells exactly like tangerines

the seahorse isn't a real horse
of course you know that but
it looks like ones some people say
I'm not a boy because I look
away because I say I wish I was
a seahorse underwater wings
and color changing and carried by
the sea some people say I am
more seahorse than me I say
sometimes the ocean looks full
of a **millionbillion** seahorses all
trying hard to hide but you
never can hide all the way away

my mom said don't always go on
about seahorses say **hellogoodbye**
say the weather feels nice today
which is boring and maybe you
might like seahorses or want to
learn about them no she says
anything else anything which leaves
infinity too many choices so you
should pick say spiral notebooks
or the end of the world did you
know if the oceans don't boil
212 degrees on the fahrenheit scale
seahorses might survive without us

today we practice asking questions
how big is it is it green how does
that make you feel your turn she said
but I don't want a turn **don'twant**
to ask questions that I could
just look the answers up on my own
but how do we look up the way
sally is feeling she says I don't know
I said look up she says and see
for yourself can you please ask
a question why are we doing this I say

the moon is the ocean's clock
mom says she said the world is
like a clock spinning too fast
but she knows that's ridiculous
because the world spins so slow
you can't even tell it's spinning
she says a lot of ridiculous
things that I'm her baby boy
and **stopthatpleasestopthat**
and I wish you could understand
how I feel sometimes I do I said
I say you feel with your hands
yes she says yes of course you do

the seahorse can hardly swim though
it lives in the ocean and has fins
it's mostly carried by the tides or
tied to seagrasses the same
color as its skin I don't know *who*
sailed to sea and he told us of his why
it would live somewhere it's not
good at getting around in or even how
it survived forever without growing
bigger and bigger fins but it did because
it has a **handtail** always holding
on and anyway if it was different
it wouldn't be a seahorse anymore

tell me about your friends she says
she says a friend is someone you like
to be around no not seahorses
exactly she said someone who can
like you back yes your brother might
be a friend your mother maybe
but who else Jacques Cousteau I say
french naval officer explorer scientist
we'd stay under for hours where
the dark hides its **secretcreatures**
I know he knows every species of
seahorse and how they hide but does he
like you back she says mom does
she likes me back she sometimes
calls me her little Jacques Cousteau

weather wrecks everything here grays
wood in weeks for years twists
pines into poses you can hold
only a second or two before you fall
get up anthony says or I'm leaving
you here but he won't because
mom said I couldn't be alone anymore
on the beach because the tidepools
memorize me and the riptides are quick
kill 100.6 people a year worldwide
they tick the tidepools mom says
but really they just empty out and
fill in again not like clocks at all
except sometimes they're round just
empty and full like **mudbathtubs**
don't even think about it anthony says

I like tangerines no. 2 pencils sharpened
to perfect points I like the call of geese
unseeable above clouds the names
of tropical fish I like the feel of steel
wool of cellophane the feeling of entering
water the same hotness as my skin
I almost can't feel it just the tug of
the tide pulling pulling back into itself *and he*
told us of his life in the land of submarines
the sound of the ocean drowning
everything out I like to go under and see
what lives there but mom doesn't like that

how was it Jacques diving under
the first time deeper each time
could you understand your eyes Jacques
it was all yours every creature and
their secrets suddenly yours you said
you wanted to stay under forever
to live deeper and study the black
with the **aqualung** on your back
you said that man has only to sink
beneath the surface and he is free
but too far and he risks rapture
or a ruptured tank you said I think
I could stay under forever Jacques
sometimes it's hard to breathe up here

today we practice telling jokes but
I don't know why the chicken
crossed the road unless there is a fox
chasing him or a bucket of seed
on the other side it's funny she says
laughing but if the chicken got hit
by a truck that wouldn't be funny
because roadkill never makes anyone
laugh except maybe ants maybe
because they're happy about the meat
but happy and funny are not quite
the same are happy and funny the same
I say **knockknock** she says who's there
but how was I supposed to know

this is my collection of **brokenmachines**
though they weren't all broken before
I unscrew the faces unmake them piece
by piece gearwheel from pinion from
rod from spring each useless without
the others but always I could put them
back together to make new machines
any apparatus consisting of interrelated parts
or all of them in one giant machine which
could figure out pi to a billion places
or translate dolphin or fill the world
with three and a half seconds of silence

anthony said snap out of it says you can't
just stare into space and with the clouds
right now he's right the sky is **allwhite**
and the sun only a brighter white stop tripping
out anthony says we've got shit to do
but really he just wants to stand outside
the dairy queen and talk to girls and then
he's happy to have me quiet and staring
and so we sailed on to the sun until we found
this is my brother he says he's special
he says that sucks she tells him yeah
he said sometimes it's pretty hard on me
but already the clouds are starting to clear

if you put an ocean seahorse in a tank
it usually dies because the water
is too watery and besides there aren't tides
inside a fish tank I think I'd like my own
seahorse but not the ones they grow
in pet stores I don't like ferrets because
they're sneaky and squeaking always
figuring their way out mom said I can
have a bunny but bunnies can't swim
very well I think and bunnies are gay too
anthony says watch your mouth mom says
should I take my eyes out he says
and **laughsnorts** and it's funny because
he's right I should remember that joke

we are all detectives she said searching
for clues deciphering signs the conversion
of code into concrete language if the sky
is dark and everyone is running for shelter
if the bowl is empty and your dog
is scratching the door what does it mean
she said I don't have a dog I say
is this a **trickquestion** I say you sit down
she says next to your best friend but
he moves away you say hello and he says
nothing what does it mean can you read
the signs what does it mean if you
come home and find your mother crying
in the kitchen your father's closet empty

I like the sound of yelling **faraway**
the sound of playing doors I slam
doors sometimes to calm myself
I slide them in how they fit perfectly
each key in its lock one key one
shape mated the locksmith said
to its keyhole and the sound of keys
tinking from my belt as I wander
the neighborhood wondering what's
behind each door wishing I had
more keys a key for every door a key
to open everything to keep it shut

mom says the leaves eat light she says
the names of everything are made up
are nicknames we'll never really know
she says this place it would've been
on the bottom of the ocean our house
overflowed by water by years of leagues
mesopelagic bathypelagic abyssopelagic
she says it's not my fault it's no one's
that without wind the birds would fall
from the sky our voices wouldn't carry
as far as we need them to and the light
that we see by is dead she says you
can't be courageous unless you're afraid
she says she's courageous every day

there's one thing I don't understand
Jacques how does the sea cast
a spell I don't know much
about wizards but they're people
at least a fisherman casts a line into
the sea *the sea of green and we lived*
beneath the waves to catch a fish a big fish
if his line is long and he's lucky
but he can't see under the surface
of the sea can't know what
he's caught until it's **overwater**
I heard them say it once hey can you
take the line a spell but Jacques
he just stood there like the other one
and nothing happened so I left

it doesn't hurt as much as you
would think it's just the blood comes
so suddenly at first the throbbing
and my heart **toofast** I never
even ever thought to hit him back
roundhouse uppercut left hook
because the laughing because
the crowd so close was worse than
punches so close I couldn't think of
anything but running home
did you cry anthony says no I say
I bled nice work champ he says
I'll beat his face tomorrow and he did

people on tv are crying again because
the toothpaste is gone or someone
died my aunt died when I was thirteen
and a woman sang such a long song
in french or italian and everyone cried
humans are the only species to shed tears
I was **sortofsad** too because my shoes
were too tight and they hurt and the crows
cawed so loud I couldn't concentrate
couldn't figure out the words she was
singing why no one was bleeding but
everyone kept crying and crying I don't
even think my mom knows italian

if divers shine **waterlights** on them
they remember back to shadows escape
into the coral or seagrass where if
they clench their eyes you won't find
them I heard them yelling for me
so long I hid so well they yelled and
yelled but I shut my eyes and sat so
quiet so tight inside the toy chest
inside the dark inside my chest no lights
could even find me I coughed once
but the sirens were too loud to hear

there are places so dark at the bottom
of the ocean the fish don't have eyes
they just float around feeling for
the slightest shiver then they know
something is there I don't know
if they know what it is or just open
their mouths wide and swallow the dark
angler gaper fangtooth coffinfish
or swim the other way which is what
they must have a million years ago
to escape something deadly in the light
and they like it there in the dark
and got so good at **notseeing**
now they'll never leave now they're
just one more darkness among many

the clouds right now are cumulonimbus
which means a storm soon rain
like cats and dogs mom says which
means she said a lot of rain
to bring the cats and dogs inside
and our friends are all aboard many more
of them I guess so they can watch the clouds
with us grow and grow darker you can
hear it already the first fat drops
falling **overthere** the sky so dark it looks
like night showed up too early
there's nothing now but the pounding
rain on the roof my mom yelling
close the windows close the windows

sometimes a shock runs through me
a wave runs through me and
I surface a moment bobbing up
and down feeling the whole
ocean with my **toetips** and almost
I think I could figure you out
could say hello into your eyes
say do you like seahorses
hello there hi do you like seahorses

I built one once from two two liters
and a length of hose a little duct tape
and a pair of ski goggles it worked
as long as I didn't breathe but then
the water rushing so fast and me
coughing out the sea the taste of salt
approximately 3.6 percent by weight
it wasn't really an aqualung but I
wore it a week anyway to school
the halls **orangecolored** and the taste
of salt still in the hose how they all
aparted when I walked down the hall
the way you never can touch a school
of fish how they slip always just out
of reach until anthony tore it off
jesus he said give yourself a chance

are there species Jacques even you
don't know that hide so well so deep
they might as well not exist it's hard
to believe but maybe one tiny
snackfish learning how to survive
on trash to eat banana peels and gasoline
it is not the strongest who will survive
but those who can manage change
so in a thousand years we won't
even recognize it won't have a name
I wish I could talk to you Jacques
I don't know why people like chainsaws
and roller skates and cauliflower
there must be one tiny or too quick
hidden so well so long we wouldn't
even know if it disappeared right now

today we practice reading emotions
but not the same as books we
look for clues in the upturned corners
of lips in eyes **squeezedtight**
surprise she says is an open mouth
anger a shut one boredom
a slouch like shame but somewhat
differently she said white knuckles
wandering eyes she says I can tell
you are confused by the way
you tilt your head did you hear
what your body just said good then
do anticipation do guilt show me
how it feels to finally understand

frogs aren't full of **clockparts** guts
were everywhere in little cups and
only I wanted to get closer to see the tiny
heart the thick black liver to trace each
vein back to its start let everyone see
the teacher says but I can't trace them all
all the way back can't separate each
part as neatly as a clock it's time to go
he says muscle from tendon from cartilage
from bone but the blood the human
body contains nearly six quarts isn't so
easy to separate it's time he says if only
I had more time if we could freeze it

the sun arrives too many strangers
crowds the beach with frisbee dogs
and people and blankets and sand
castles with crooked walls my habitat
taken over I saw it once a movie
about the **greatbarrierreef** about
all the species living there on top
of each other *many more of them live
next door* an eel in every crack
the fish almost bumping into each
other even the coral is alive so many
fathoms of ocean empty and all
that life crowded so close but I
guess the kites are kind of beautiful

you're a good listener you never say
a word never even stare off into
space or get out of your chair I bet
you're never in trouble I swam once
so far out I couldn't hear my mom
yelling she said she was yelling but
I was underwater past the waves
where the water is calm where the fish
school just beyond the breaking
waves I was looking for fish when
the **wholeworld** went quiet I couldn't
hear my mom or the waves it is
so quiet I listened and listened
but all I could hear was my heart

anthony says it's my fault says he left
because I'm such a spaz because
I couldn't speak in straight lines or
sometimes at all because I screamed
the nights awake he says or stayed
so quiet so long anthony says he left
a long time before he finally left
down at the beach for hours or gone
driving his chevy when he really left
he left an oil stain **sixfeetwide** across
the driveway it looks like a country
anthony says like china or antarctica
the earth's southernmost continent
he's probably living there he says
living somewhere so far he'll never
find his way all the way back to here

when I was young younger when
I was **stuckstill** by the urge just now
to disappear inside my head inside
the clocks I sometimes take apart
to see what makes them tick to stop
time and how the gears tooth
into each other so exactly without
a slip without a sound they eat
time mom says the way I eat
a pickle sandwich in seventeen bites
three minutes three gearwheels
one mainspring a pendulum less than
it seems it takes to make a man

he didn't really mean you're a genius
anthony says he was just messing
with you it's sarcasm dumb ass
sarcasm I say like when someone
says nice shot jordan chicago bulls
shooting guard 1984 to 1999* when you
just **airballed** he says you know
I don't play basketball I say jesus
it's just an example go look it up
in the dictionary he says good idea
I say jesus why are you so smart
at some stuff and so stupid at others
I know pi to one hundred places
yeah like he said you're a real genius

the waves are too high today to swim
through feel shoved against my chest
my chin lifting me a little bit off
the ground and down again the horizon
disappeared with each rise goodbye
goodbye you should say when someone
leaves shake hands high five pleased
to meet you waves I wave and lift
and the band begins to play as I rise
heavyless a moment again buoyed
I heard the man say once carried
they carried a girl blue as the ocean
to the ambulance gone mom says
but I could still see her feet goodbye

I'll find one once all my own but not
where you'd think not copying coral
or hiding with its eyes shut just drifting
out into open water an unknown
species of seahorse in stripes of blue
in shades of seawater so you can't see it
unfindable among the fathoms except
for one **blackspot** one tiny mark
to make it easy prey but he'll be there
anyway carried by the current carried
north and south past every open mouth
but still I'll find him and call him
secret blue little aqualung I'll hold him
a moment in my hand then let go
my one last the miraculous courageous

they're not helpless they can hide
so still and surprise their prey
pretend to be a strip of kelp
or move so slow through water
they make no waves no signs then
suckdown tiny crustaceans
in one bite it's easy as pie
mom says easy as falling off a bike
which I have and it was easy
anthony says they're little ninjas
clans of mercenaries in feudal Japan
the way they sneak up on things
and kapow swallow it whole
it's almost kind of cool he says
which is I think almost kind of cool

goldfish don't have memories
they wake up each day to a new
world mom says I have to name it
but how will he remember
his name I say or who I am
turtles can remember a thousand
miles across the sea **returnback**
to exactly the spot they were born
thirty-seven steps from here
to the frontdoor three minutes twelve
seconds to the shore if you run
if the tide is in and there's no wind
I think I'll name him Jacques

the trees outside my window scratch
the glass I like the sound sometimes
sometimes I open the window and step
out onto the tree into the branches
where no one knows my secret
hideout in the tangle of branches
my world of leaves of light *we*
all live in a yellow through the leaves
and then the wind coming in in
waves like water waves but they're not I
feel it sometimes like I could be
a real seahorse a **treehorse** maybe
but of course I'm always still myself

in another memory my brother slips
his arm around my neck chokes
my throat to lift me off the floor look
at me he's saying he's yelling look
at me but the tracks aren't quite
right quite straight so the train
the golden spike was driven may 1869
slipcatches each time it rounds
the bend the wheels spinning look
he says in my eyes in my eyes
he said holding my face in his hands
the train slipping again I can
fix it he says I'm gonna punch you
in the face if you don't look at me
he said the train is off the tracks again

freshwater tiger tail thorny
brazilian shortsnouted dwarf
narrow-bellied hedgehog
zebra lichtenstein's reef
weedy three-spotted pony
longnosed bargibant's black
knobby paradoxical pigmy
big belly calidonian bullneck
reunion **saltwhite** banded
common japanese red
spiny false-eyed winged
the great the crowned the sad

we are making a memory mom says we are
staring at the waves coming in at the
crabs **sidewayswalking** along the beach
remember each piece she said the ships
out there the driftwood at our feet remember
each thing as if it is a piece of furniture
and this a room place it piece by piece
she says in a room in your mind the gulls
crying the fisherman unloading their catch
the scent of salt and the sound of the surf
arriving each time remember the shades
of sunset and how close we are right now
memorize the warmth of your hand in mine
how darkness turns the lighthouse on

anthony said a man talks with his fists
fights fast takes no shit anthony
says he's the **manofthehouse**
and for fighting he is but always
he's in trouble for it mom yelling
but he never tries to fight her back
just takes it staring at his shoes
shame is denoted by a downward gaze
I saw him crying once after
so maybe he can be a boy and a man
the way mom says flower means
both rose and to grow means
he can talk with his fists and mouth
but what is he when he's silent

today we practice listening keeping
our eyes up keeping our hands
unflapping in our laps the answer is
the squareroot of seven the answer is
chlorophyll I'm over here she
said what's the question I say
there is no question I want to know
that you're listening she says I am
I say but how can you show me
she says where should your eyes be
on my face I said where should we
be looking when we are listening
to someone she says can you please
look at me in the eyes she says yes

impossible notions are the only ones
to succeed you said but Jacques
the impossible is impossible or else
it's not I've tried two-hundred seventeen
times to stay under on my own
stayed until my chest burned but Jacques
three minutes fifty-two seconds
is my best and almost I **blackedout**
in a yellow submarine yellow submarine
not rapture quite but a feeling like
the ocean was in my body was my body
a feeling like up was down so I swam
down and down until I saw the light

who knows why they're called hands
they hold nothing don't even
have fingers and how could you
hold time anyway a whole day
in one hand the night another
the light is light enough but impossible
to hold hold on mom says
but means wait not find a handle
I can handle it she also says
but mostly when she can't when I
come home and she's crying
saying it's ok honey **it'llbeok**
I just need a minute but always
I count to sixty and still she's crying

my **shirttag** is the only thought
I can think sometimes I can't think
until I rip it out remove that rub
the somatic system regulates tactile
stimulation that rubs me the wrong way
maybe I'm doomed or the world is
all out of comfortable shirts
there's a reason animals don't
wear clothes except for little dogs
or circus bears but they wouldn't
if they could choose I wouldn't
if I could choose but sometimes
you have to grin and bear it
mom says even though I know
bears only have to wear little hats

the bluffs are covered with names
of people I don't know hearts
and plus signs scratched into
the **windpackedsand** with sticks
anthony carved SUCK IT six feet high
and after chucked rocks at birds
I wish you weren't autistic sometimes
he says but at least you're not
an asshole I didn't say something back
I've learned it's better that way
and besides the waves were too loud
a big storm coming in so we ran
home all the way with thunder
six seconds apart and quick locked
the door I didn't mean it he said

something in the light in the way
the light sometimes surprises
the lightest light you've ever seen
so bright you want a different
name for it how you can almost
hear someone calling your name
but the light is louder so bright
you can't see anything *every one of us has*
all we need which makes me wonder
is it light at all if it doesn't help you
see you see if you just sideways
your eyes just right the world is
light the world looks disappearing
and if you can hold it **slantwise**
in your sight it might really forever

are you ever lonely Jacques below
the waves she says when you're alone
enough you're lonely but I'm never
lonely Jacques with doors and clocks
and the whole ocean to keep me
thinking with the rough of starfish
and rain on garbagecan lids with light
through the leaves making shapes
on the sidewalk I could trace them all
trace one a thousand times to get it
right she can't be right about it Jacques
about loneliness with gearwheels
and tangerines with **ceilingfans** and
the silver paper they wrap gum in
I couldn't be lonely not with anthony
and mom not with seahorses Jacques

every clock in the house shines
a different time I don't know which
one is right if any or maybe none
except the moon which I know
isn't full of gears silicon magnesium
iron aluminum but keeps perfect
time it's a **stateofmind** mom says
like oregon I say it's whatever
you make of it she tells me but
that can't be right because the moon
outside the window is full keeps
keeping its secret time it's getting
late she says it's time to go to sleep

the gulls make circles over nothing
all day drift higher or out to sea
without moving their wings like kites
without strings a man says passing
by and good morning he said
though it's six past twelve almost
time for the tide to go to leave
jellyfish stranded and shells for the old
folks to bend **onehandonaknee**
down so slowly and pick up for me
to search for eels or anemones
or anything else that can't escape
the lowspots I remember him
searching hours for agates staring
through whole afternoons at his shoes

I would be green the **yellowygreen**
of avocados inside I could hide
up in the leaves and never be seen
so genius to blend in to show
fear in a flash of really red a splatter
of aquamarine to wrap yourself
in the color of yourself and be
unseen *sky of blue sea of green* if only
we were seahorses if we could
change colors instead of clothes
emotions across our skin how easy
then to read someone to know
what's in their head to know who
wants you gone and who wants you

amazing they don't get pulverized
just a few thin plates to protect
against the sea the rocks I dropped
one once a plate to see it shatter
scatter across the floor I threw it
against the floor to watch it crack
back to a billion pieces the crash
then everything **soquiet** listening we
found a piece three years later
under the refrigerator general electric
4.5 cu ft PPLZ43D2Y the whole time
hiding how else could they survive
hiding in the seagrass in their plates
for years hiding so tiny hearts

I did it last night in the bathtub Jacques
stayed under until everything turned
black until mom pulled me out
and kissed me back into the bathroom
I told her to stop and stop crying
she was heavy on my chest my chest
so full of breath like big waves she
held me so long but it was nice
a moment to be a fish not fighting
for air everything was lights staring
upthrough the water everything wasn't
quite itself did you know Jacques
there are fish that can breathe on land
for up to hours but of course you do

today we practice saying goodbye
leaving the conversation at the right
moment it was nice to meet you
we should talk again **shakehands**
she says smile she says so they know
you're happy but what if I'm not
when we leave we smile so that
we leave a good impression tidepools
are impressions isolated by ebbing tides
we are practicing leaving not talking
about tidepools she says we don't
start a conversation when we see
someone wants to say goodbye
we smile we shake we leave a good
impression with an eel in it I said

the ocean takes an inch each year
unbuilds the beach each day gives
it back mom says the ocean is full
of gifts and dangers the world
is a beached whale sometimes
I asked but she wouldn't explain
said only sometimes there's nothing
anyone can do but carry buckets
from the sea nothing to do but
wait and see if the tide comes in
did it I asked did it what she said
did the tide come in in time but
she's just silent and looking out at
the waves awhile it will she says

last night I dreamed I was a seahorse
seethrough blue a black coronet
but when I woke I wasn't the seahorse
had gone in the ocean it's like that
always just holding on a swell from
somewhere a big boat going bye
and you think there's no way he can
hold on and he can't and he lets
go gets washed along with the tide
his little fins useless unless
he doesn't fight it he doesn't try to
break the course but buoys on
the wake just let's himself be taken
along away until the ocean pours
his body back into the world and he
lived beneath the waves in our yellow submarine

Acknowledgments

I'd like to thank Jon Thompson for his faith in this book, and for publishing a selection of these poems in *Free Verse*. My gratitude to the Dorothy Sargent Rosenberg Foundation and the Elizabeth George Foundation for funding that allowed me to complete this project.

Thanks to Beth Spencer, Harvey Hix, Carolina Ebeid, Rebecca Starks, Beth Stanley, Nicole Cullen and Ryan Cannon for their insights and encouragement. To Kristin, always, for her patience and sanity. To Porter and Cora, for their endless curiosity.

Thank you to the kids and families I've had the pleasure of serving, for all you've taught me.

Free Verse Editions

Edited by Jon Thompson

Pilgrimly by Siobhán Scarry

Poems from above the Hill & Selected Work by Ashur Etwebi, translated by Brenda Hillman & Diallah Haidar

The Prison Poems by Miguel Hernández, translated by Michael Smith

Puppet Wardrobe by Daniel Tiffany

Quarry by Carolyn Guinzio

remanence by Boyer Rickel

Rumor by Elizabeth Robinson

Signs Following by Ger Killeen

Split the Crow by Sarah Sousa

Spine by Carolyn Guinzio

Spool by Matthew Cooperman

Summoned by Guillevic, translated by Monique Chefdor & Stella Harvey

Sunshine Wound by L. S. Klatt

System and Population by Christopher Sindt

These Beautiful Limits by Thomas Lisk

They Who Saw the Deep by Geraldine Monk

The Thinking Eye by Jennifer Atkinson

This History That Just Happened by Hannah Craig

An Unchanging Blue: Selected Poems 1962–1975 by Rolf Dieter Brinkmann, translated by Mark Terrill

Under the Quick by Molly Bendall

Verge by Morgan Lucas Schuldt

The Wash by Adam Clay

We'll See by Georges Godeau, translated by Kathleen McGookey

What Stillness Illuminated by Yermiyahu Ahron Taub

Winter Journey [Viaggio d'inverno] by Attilio Bertolucci, translated by Nicholas Benson

Wonder Rooms by Allison Funk

About the Author

Josh Booton's first book, *The Union of Geometry & Ash*, was awarded the Dorothy Brunsman Poetry Prize. His work has been supported by grants from The University of Texas at Austin, the Dorothy Sargent Rosenberg Foundation and the Elizabeth George Foundation. He lives in Boise, Idaho, where he works with children and teens with autism spectrum disorder as a pediatric speech therapist.

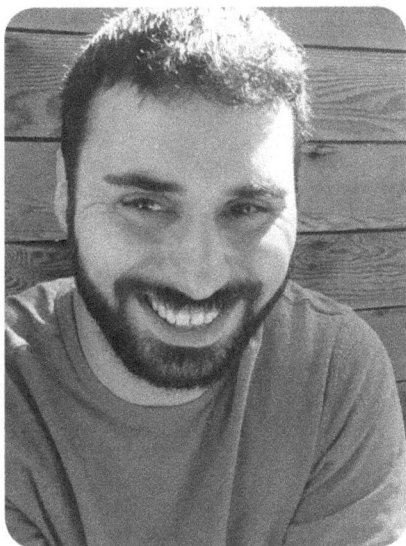

Photograph of the author by K. Schultz.
Used by permission.

www.ingramcontent.com/pod-product-compliance
Lightning Source LLC
Chambersburg PA
CBHW022039090426
42741CB00007B/1129